Bridge the Gap
Understanding Generational Communication Differences

Table of Contents

1. Introduction 1
2. Setting the Scene: A Generational Overview 2
   2.1. Baby Boomers: Post-War Optimism and Growth 2
   2.2. Generation X: Balancing Tradition and Modernity 2
   2.3. Millennials: Digital Pioneers Seeking Purpose 3
   2.4. Generation Z: True Digital Natives in a Fast-Paced World 3
3. Baby Boomers: Communicating with Tradition 5
   3.1. Engaging with Direct Communication 5
   3.2. Focusing on Professionalism 5
   3.3. Open to Learning New Technologies 6
   3.4. Working within Defined Boundaries 6
   3.5. Value Experiences and Loyalty 6
   3.6. The Gift of Time 7
4. Gen X: The Bridge Between Two Worlds 8
   4.1. Gen X: An Introduction 8
   4.2. Influences on Gen X Communication 8
   4.3. Communication in the Workplace 9
   4.4. The Digital Evolution and Gen X 9
   4.5. Communication With Millennials and Gen Z 10
   4.6. Balancing Act: Gen X Techniques 10
   4.7. The Power and Potential of Gen X 11
   4.8. Gen X: The Silent Connectors 11
5. Millennials: Digital Pioneers in a Connected World 12
   5.1. Communication Style and Mediums 12
   5.2. The Impact of Technology 13
   5.3. Understanding Millennial Subgroups 13
   5.4. Keys to Communicating with Millennials 14
   5.5. Building Bridges with Millennials 14

6. Gen Z: The Trendsetters of Modern Communication 16
    6.1. The Rise of Digital Natives 16
    6.2. The Speed of Communication 16
    6.3. Embracing Non-Verbal Communication 17
    6.4. The Impact of Social Media 17
    6.5. Realigning Privacy Concerns 17
    6.6. Understanding the Omnichannel Approach 18
7. Navigating Intergenerational Misunderstandings 19
    7.1. Baby Boomers: The Communicative Traditionalists 19
    7.2. Generation X: The Independent Innovators 20
    7.3. Millennials: The Digital Conversationalists 20
    7.4. Gen Z: The Tech-Innate Catalysts 21
    7.5. Techniques to Navigate Misunderstandings 21
8. Fostering Empathy Across the Generations 23
    8.1. The Importance of Empathy in Cross-Generational
    Communication 23
    8.2. Developing Empathetic Awareness 24
    8.3. Understanding Generational Experiences 24
    8.4. Bridges, Not Walls: Encouraging Open Dialogue 25
    8.5. The Power of Storytelling 25
9. Developing Effective Communication Strategies 27
    9.1. Understanding the Gen Z 27
    9.2. Engaging Millennials 28
    9.3. Reaching Out to Gen X 28
    9.4. Communicating with Baby Boomers 29
    9.5. Cross-Generational Communication Strategies 29
10. Harmonizing the Multi-generational Workplace 31
    10.1. Recognizing Unique Generational Traits 31
    10.2. Communication: The Crucial Connector 32
    10.3. Creating an Inclusive Environment 33

- 10.4. Encouraging Cross-generational Mentoring ... 33
- 10.5. Leveraging Generational Strengths ... 33
- 10.6. Responding to Conflict ... 34
- 11. Towards a Unified Future: Appreciating the Value of Each Generation ... 35
  - 11.1. Understanding Generational Values ... 35
  - 11.2. Embracing Differences, Enhancing Collaboration ... 36
  - 11.3. Each Generation Has a Unique Strength ... 36
  - 11.4. Encouraging Generational Knowledge Transfer ... 36
  - 11.5. Fostering an Inclusive Workplace Environment ... 37
  - 11.6. Bridging the Gap: The Role of Leadership ... 37
  - 11.7. The Synergy of Generational Diversity ... 37

Chapter 1. Introduction

Welcome to our Special Report, "Bridge the Gap: Understanding Generational Communication Differences"! This illuminating report isn't your run-of-the-mill, stuffy analysis. Oh no, it's an enthralling exploration that will leap off the pages and guide you on an engaging journey through time! We'll navigate the varying communication styles of Baby Boomers, Gen X, Millennials, and Gen Z, showcasing the unique strengths and challenges of each, while also providing practical solutions to improve your cross-generational communication skills. Communication mishaps within families, workplaces, and communities will become a thing of the past with this knowledge at your fingertips! So grab our report, buckle up, and get ready to embark on a radiant voyage of understanding and connection, where bridging the generational gap provides not only insight and empathy, but also paves the way for stronger relationships! Be prepared – your view on generational communication differences is about to be revolutionized!

Chapter 2. Setting the Scene: A Generational Overview

The understanding of generational gaps begins with an overview of the four main generational categories. Each generation is shaped by the unique social, economic, political, and technological circumstances of its formative years, resulting in distinct attitudes, behaviors, and communication styles.

2.1. Baby Boomers: Post-War Optimism and Growth

Born from 1946 to 1964, following the end of World War II, Baby Boomers grew up during a time of remarkable economic growth, social change, and newfound optimism. They witnessed the birth of the civil rights movement, the women's liberation movement, and the counterculture of the 1960s.

In the workplace, Boomers are often characterized as ambitious, loyal, and hardworking, willing to put in long hours to climb the corporate ladder. They grew up with face-to-face communication and phone calls. As a result, they may struggle with the impersonal nature of email or instant messaging, preferring direct contact and formal communication that establishes trust and reliability.

2.2. Generation X: Balancing Tradition and Modernity

Born from 1965 to 1980, Gen Xers are the middle children of history, fixated between two influential and sizable generations – Baby Boomers and Millennials. This generation witnessed the advent of personal computers, the rise of the internet, and tumultuous geopolitical events, including the fall of the Berlin Wall and 9/11.

Gen Xers are often seen as self-reliant and independent. At work, they value skills-over-stature and seek a balance between their professional and personal lives. Their preferred communication vehicle is email – it's fast and efficient, but still provides a paper trail. They are comfortable with both direct and indirect methods of communication, often tailoring their approach according to the situation or the person they're dealing with.

2.3. Millennials: Digital Pioneers Seeking Purpose

Born from 1981 to 1996, Millennials are the first generation to grow up with the internet as part of their everyday life. They experienced monumental shifts such as the Great Recession and the Digital Revolution, profoundly impacting their communication styles, attitudes towards work, and worldviews.

Millennials are often seen as technologically savvy, diverse, educated, and globally connected. They value purpose over profit and seek meaningful work. Comfortable with digital communication platforms like social media, instant messaging, and video conference solutions, they are adept at multitasking across various modes of communication. The digital natives are less formal in their communication, often using text speak, emojis, and gifs to express themselves.

2.4. Generation Z: True Digital Natives in a Fast-Paced World

Born from 1997 to 2012, Gen Z is the first generation to grow up in a fully digital world, immersed in smartphones, social media, and streaming services from the earliest age. Occurrences such as the

Global Financial Crisis, Climate Change, and the COVID-19 pandemic have shaped their views and behaviors.

Gen Z is pragmatic, diverse, entrepreneurial, and passionate about social issues. This generation values authenticity and transparency, preferring communication channels that deliver this, such as personal video content and interactive stories. Being digital natives, they navigate fluidly between channels for different purposes.

In summary, understanding generational differences is not about creating divisions but rather acknowledging diversity. However, it's crucial to remember that not everyone in a generation behaves homogeneously. These are general patterns that can guide us in understanding better and bridging the communication gap between generations. Understanding each generation's formative influences, characteristics, and preferences can help us to develop strategies that foster effective cross-generational communication.

After all, every person, regardless of their generation, wants to be understood, acknowledged, and valued. A thorough investigation of generational communication differences provides us just one more tool in that endeavor.

Chapter 3. Baby Boomers: Communicating with Tradition

Baby Boomers, born between 1946 and 1964, witnessed a significant amount of change in their time, from the Civil Rights movement to the breakthrough of the internet age. Communicating with those from the Baby Boomer generation can appear to be complex, especially with the varying communication styles now available. But rest assured, there are several traditional methods that can improve the communication experience between Boomers and other generations.

3.1. Engaging with Direct Communication

Boomers grew up during a time when face-to-face or over-the-phone discussions were prevalent. Unlike many of today's digital natives, they did not grow up hiding behind screens, and hence, they value direct, personal communication. They appreciate and are more comfortable in situations where issues and ideas are discussed openly. When dealing with Boomers, try to prioritize these in-person or direct forms of communication as it fosters an atmosphere of mutual respect and trust.

3.2. Focusing on Professionalism

Professionalism carries a significant amount of weight in Boomer communication. They tend to be formal in office settings and follow a hierarchical structure when it comes to their conversations. This stems from their traditional upbringing where respect and order were highly valued. Even emails should be written with a bit more formality and keep to the point. Avoid using abbreviated forms of words or emojis, which can be seen as unprofessional.

3.3. Open to Learning New Technologies

While it may be true that Boomers didn't grow up with the internet and smartphones, it doesn't mean they are technologically inept. On the contrary, many Boomers have actively embraced technology and learned to adapt to the digital age. Teaching technology can be an effective method of fostering better communication, but patience, understanding, and clear instructions are key during the learning process.

3.4. Working within Defined Boundaries

Boundaries are crucial when communicating with a Boomer. This generation tends to value their free time and separates work from home life. Boomers may not always appreciate receiving work-related messages or calls outside of work hours. Maintain these boundaries to ensure a smoother communication and relationship with them.

3.5. Value Experiences and Loyalty

Boomers are a generation that values loyalty, hard work, and respect for authority. Recognizing and appreciating these values will go a long way in strengthening communication. Conversations that allow Boomers to share their experiences, wisdom, and insights are often appreciated.

3.6. The Gift of Time

With age comes wisdom and patience. Boomers often prefer taking time during discussions and decision-making processes. This slower pace allows for comprehensive exploration of ideas and minimizes misunderstandings. When communicating with this generation, don't rush them. Give them the time they need, and you'll find the results rewarding.

In summary, successful communication with Baby Boomers relies heavily on directness, professionalism, patience, boundary respect, and the acknowledgment of their wisdom and experiences. By understanding these points, one can facilitate smoother conversations, fostering enhanced connectivity, trust, and mutual respect.

As society evolves, technology improves, and communication styles shift, Boomers have indeed shown a willingness to adapt. However, their traditional communication methods still play a major role in their interactions. By acknowledging and respecting these values, we can bridge the generational gap and foster an environment of understanding and cooperation. Despite the Boomers' preference for tradition, their acceptance and adaptation to change showcases their resilience and tenacity. This balance between tradition and modernity is what makes Baby Boomers a fascinating generation to communicate with.

Chapter 4. Gen X: The Bridge Between Two Worlds

Generationally positioned between the post-war optimism and exuberance of the Baby Boomers and the disrupting innovativeness of the Millennials and Gen Z, Generation X has often been characterized as the "middle child". Gen X, those born between 1965 and 1980, have quietly but significantly bridged two radically different eras of communication and forged their own unique practices in the process.

4.1. Gen X: An Introduction

Just like their namesake, Gen X occupies an intriguing crossroads in time – one that links the technological advancements and social changes of the 20th and 21st centuries. Many of them witnessed the transition from manual typewriters to personal computers, from rotary dial telephones to smartphones – essentially, they've seen the shift from wired to wireless communication.

While they may not always be the most flashy or vocal generation, their impact on society, particularly on communication styles, continues to play a vital and often overlooked role.

4.2. Influences on Gen X Communication

Drawing from their temporal position and the sociocultural factors that shaped their formative years, Gen Xers exhibit distinctive communication styles. They are realists, skeptics, autonomous, and incredibly adaptable – traits that largely stem from their experiences during their formative years.

Growing up during a time of economic downturn, rising divorce rates, and the emergence of the AIDS crisis, plus the fact many of them were latchkey kids because both parents were working, this generation harbors a deep sense of self-reliance, pragmatism, and resilience. They value direct, straightforward communication.

4.3. Communication in the Workplace

In the professional sphere, Gen Xers strived to be self-sufficient. They are comfortable with both traditional and digital forms of communication, making them the bridge in the workplace that typically aids understanding between older and younger generations.

Gen Xers commonly prefer a blended approach when it comes to communication channels. While they appreciate the efficiency of emails and other electronic messaging systems, they also value face-to-face communication and telephonic conversations, especially for more nuanced or critical discussions.

4.4. The Digital Evolution and Gen X

The evolution of digital technology happened in parallel with the professional lives of Gen Xers. As a result, they've watched the rise of the internet, the advent of social media, and the infiltration of smartphones in our lives.

These experiences make them unique in their understanding of both traditional and tech-driven communication forms. They remain flexible, appreciating the merits of a hand-written letter, yet fully understanding the convenience and speed of a tweet or a text message.

4.5. Communication With Millennials and Gen Z

The role Gen X plays in bridging communication gaps between other generations cannot be overstated. Gen X understands where Baby Boomers are coming from in terms of traditional communication styles. At the same time, they find common ground with Millennials and Gen Z, who lean more towards digital communication methods.

In understanding and utilizing various modes of communication across generations, Gen X exhibits patient adaptability. This adaptability is the key to their successful communication with the younger generations who rely heavily on digital modes and the older generations who may still prefer analog methods.

Given their unique vantage point, Gen X may also play a significant role in alleviating the intergenerational communication issues that often plague organizations.

4.6. Balancing Act: Gen X Techniques

In creating their unique communication style, Gen X mastered the art of balancing. They maintain the fine line between formal and informal communication. They know when to send a quick instant message and when a face-to-face meeting is more effective. Even in their use of humor, Gen X tends to balance workplace communication by being masters of subtle sarcasm that is not overly offensive.

4.7. The Power and Potential of Gen X

Generationally speaking, institutions should be leveraging the experiences and adaptive communication skills of Gen X. Their breadth and depth of understanding, coupled with their flexibility, gives them the potential to be brokers and facilitators of meaningful and effective dialogue that can address inter-communications issues.

In this context, Gen X should be encouraged to play a more proactive role in bridging generational communication gaps by sharing their skills, knowledge, and experiences.

4.8. Gen X: The Silent Connectors

In conclusion, Gen X, though often overshadowed by the more exuberant Boomers or the techie Millennials and Gen Z, possesses unique characteristics that play a crucial role in the maze of generational communication. Their life experiences and adaptability to situations make them the perfect fulcrum of balance and understanding, bridging the communication gap between generations.

Appreciating Gen X and their contribution to effective communication is crucial to enhancing overall communication dynamics and fostering stronger relationships, whether within families, workplaces, or broader communities. Their unique position serves as an essential bridge between different worlds. And while Gen X may not be the loudest across the generational divide, their influence and potential speak volumes.

Chapter 5. Millennials: Digital Pioneers in a Connected World

In an ever-evolving digital landscape, the Millennial generation emerges as pioneers, shaping and embracing novel ways of communicating. Born between the early 1980s and the mid-1990s, Millennials have witnessed the rise of the internet, the explosion of social media, and the ubiquitous adoption of smartphones, becoming key players in this digitally connected world.

5.1. Communication Style and Mediums

Millennials' communication style is characterized by their affinity for digital tools, from emails and text messaging to social media platforms such as Facebook, Twitter, Instagram, and LinkedIn. They not only utilize these tools for social interaction but also as critical channels for seeking information, shopping, performing work tasks, and more.

Platform	Usage
—	Email
Millennial's preferred medium for professional communication. It's official, reliable and asynchronous nature caters to the Millennial's love for flexibility and multitasking.	—

Platform	Usage
Text messaging	This medium offers immediacy and convenience for quick, less formal interactions, often supplemented with emojis or GIFs providing added layers of emotional nuance.
—	Social media

5.2. The Impact of Technology

Thanks to their digital fluency, Millennials have brought several trends to life, including digital nomadism, remote working, and the gig economy. At the same time, their heavy reliance on technology has drawbacks as well, leading to concerns about the blurring line between work and personal life, cyberbullying, and screen addiction.

5.3. Understanding Millennial Subgroups

While it's easy to stereotype Millennials as an overarching group, doing so risks overlooking the significant differences within the generation. Consider, for example, the difference between Older Millennials, who came of age using dial-up internet and flip phones, and Younger Millennials, for whom smartphones and fast, always-on internet access were a given from an early age.

5.4. Keys to Communicating with Millennials

While keeping in mind that there's considerable variation within any group, here are a few tips that generally hold true when communicating with Millennials:

- Value their input: Millennials want to know their voice is heard and their opinions are valued.
- Be genuine and transparent: Authenticity carries great weight. Millennials can easily detect sugar-coated information and excessive corporate jargon.
- Make it quick and interactive: Brevity is the soul of Millennial communication. They favor concise, meaningful exchanges over lengthy declarations.

5.5. Building Bridges with Millennials

Despite stereotypes portraying Millennials as tech-obsessed, this generation craves authentic relationships as much as any other. They simply use different tools to build and maintain these connections. To effectively bridge the communication gap with Millennials, resonate with their values of authenticity, inclusivity, and transparency. Indeed, by blending the digital with the personal, we can successfully communicate with Millennials, harness their strengths, and mitigate the challenges of the digital world they helped build.

This exploration into the communication habits of Millennials uncovers a generation fluent in the language of technology. It underlines a shift from the traditional face-to-face interaction towards a digital mode, which offer different forms of flexibility and exchange. Recognizing this shift is the first step towards building strong and successful symbiotic relationships across the generational divide - understanding is the key to unity.

Chapter 6. Gen Z: The Trendsetters of Modern Communication

Gen Z, those individuals born between 1997 and 2012, arrive on the scene with their own unique set of communication methods and preferences. For them, technology isn't just an everyday tool; it's intertwined with their identities and their way of life. This digital fluency sculpts their communication style and affects how they connect with other generations.

6.1. The Rise of Digital Natives

In the realm of communication, Gen Zs can certainly be tagged as the "digital natives." Unlike other generations who've witnessed gradual advancement or full-blown revolution in technology, these youngsters are born into it. They are the first generation to grow up with mobile phones, readily accessible internet, and all-knowing search engines. Rather than adopt these tools, they grow alongside them.

This ubiquitous technology usage generates an impact on how they behave, learn, and most importantly, communicate. From texting to utilizing various social media platforms, their communication styles are wrapped in digital innovation.

6.2. The Speed of Communication

One of the distinguishing characteristics of Gen Z's communication is the speed. Brought up in a world where everything is a tap or swipe away, Gen Z prides itself on quick communication. Social networks, chat apps, and video sharing platforms offer a medium for real-time dialogue and instant feedback, shaping their expectation for immediate responses.

However, the downside is that while this penchant for speed boosts efficiency, important discussions often lack depth. This lack of thorough communication could be detrimental in certain scenarios, for example, in addressing workplace issues or personal conflicts, where detailed discussions are needed.

6.3. Embracing Non-Verbal Communication

Emojis, GIFs, and memes are an integral part of Gen Z's communication arsenal. They use these as a way to add emotional context and clarify messages in non-verbal communication. While this can be confusing for older generations, Gen Z considers it an effective and fun way of expressing themselves.

6.4. The Impact of Social Media

Social media drives Gen Z's communication more than any other generation. Platforms like Snapchat, Instagram, and TikTok offer avenues of expression and connection, pushing the boundaries of conventional communication styles. User-generated content emerges as a powerful tool to voice views, influence, or simply entertain.

However, the pressure to maintain an engaging digital persona can lead to increased stress among Gen Z. FOMO (fear of missing out) is also a significant factor, and social media usage has been associated with higher levels of anxiety and loneliness among this generation.

6.5. Realigning Privacy Concerns

Contrary to previous generations' views on information sharing, Gen

Z is more cautious. They are more likely to utilize privacy settings and prefer disappearing content – Snapchat's Snaps and Stories that disappear after 24 hours are prime examples. In the wake of various scandals around data misuse, they have exhibited mounting distrust in institutions. This apprehension has significant implications on how they share and consume information.

6.6. Understanding the Omnichannel Approach

Gen Z uses multiple digital platforms simultaneously, expecting a seamless transition between each. They view communication as an omnichannel experience. So, whether they are using a mobile app, a social media platform, or a website, they expect the information and conversation threads to flow consistently across all devices.

While Gen Z's approach to communication holds a plethora of strengths, it also presents challenges when interacting with older generations less fluent in their methods. For efficient cross-generational communication, understanding and accommodating this generational perspective is key. Adopting part of their approach - like quick responses or using multiple communication channels - can also help bridge the gap. However, it's equally important for Gen Z to appreciate and learn from the communication styles of other generations.

Understanding Gen Z's communication style promises potential benefits and pitfalls. In acknowledging these, the speed of their communication can be harnessed to improve efficiency, while efforts can be made to encourage in-depth discussion where needed. Their digital-first approach can foster a greater understanding of technology across generations, while their privacy concerns can preserve respect for personal information. By bridging the perceived gap, the communicational playing field becomes all the more vibrant and inclusive.

Chapter 7. Navigating Intergenerational Misunderstandings

With the unprecedented intermingling of four generations — Baby Boomers, Gen X, Millennials, and Gen Z — in modern families, workplaces, and societies, intergenerational misunderstandings and communication hiccups have become more prevalent. The ways we communicate are intrinsically linked to our societal experiences, worldviews, and technology available during our formative years, resulting in notable generational variances in communication styles and preferences.

7.1. Baby Boomers: The Communicative Traditionalists

Representing the post-war optimism, Baby Boomers (1946-1964) grew up in a time of rapid social and economic change. They champion personal interaction and value face-to-face dialogue, evident in their propensity for meetings and one-on-one interactions within workplaces. For Baby Boomers, nothing replaces the richness of personal communication, an amalgamation of tone, facial expression, and body language. They are more formal in their communication, opting for titles and proper etiquette.

However, their preference for direct communication and sometimes skeptical views on technology can mar their understanding with younger generations who often default to digital modes.

7.2. Generation X: The Independent Innovators

Generation X (1965-1980), transitional in technological terms, experienced a time before the internet-saturation, but also witnessed and adapted to the digital revolution. Ensuing from this, Gen X embodies a blend of traditional and modern communication preferences.

The preference of Gen X leans toward email as a primary mode of communication. They appreciate the efficiency and convenience, while also adhering to a semblance of formality. A self-reliant generation, they appreciate direct, clear communication with no frills. Though technologically savvy enough to use digital platforms, they can occasionally feel overwhelmed by the obsession younger generations have with social media and instant communication.

7.3. Millennials: The Digital Conversationalists

Millennials (1981-1996), the first true digital natives, spent their formative years adapting to the crescendo of the internet and social media, resulting in a conspicuous alignment to technology-driven communication. They popularized text messaging, online chatting, and social media platforms, transforming them into essential tools for interaction.

Tech-savvy and connected, Millennials tend to favor more informal, succinct, and constant communication. However, their heavy reliance on digital tools and penchant for informality can create friction with older generations, leading to misunderstandings if not clarified.

7.4. Gen Z: The Tech-Innate Catalysts

Gen Z (1997 onwards), born into an epoch where digital tech forms the backdrop of their lives, are reshaping the communication landscape. They relish in the use of emojis, memes, and gifs to express emotions and ideas succinctly, tending to favor direct, instant communication such as DMs and text messages.

Gen Z presents a unique challenge: their digital-centric communication style confounds older generations. The dilemma lies in Gen Z's preference for brevity and visual media over detailed, text-heavy communication, which can lead to misinterpretations.

7.5. Techniques to Navigate Misunderstandings

Navigating intergenerational misunderstandings begins with awareness and empathy. Understand the communication traits of each generation, respect them, and adapt accordingly. Here are some successful strategies:

1. Listen actively and empathetically: Active listening is a cornerstone of good communication. Understand the intention behind the message, not just the words.
2. Develop versatile communication skills: Enhance your proficiency in varying modes of communication.
3. Leverage different channels: Use mixed platforms (emails, face-to-face, social media) to engage all generations.
4. Create generations-inclusive spaces: Develop environments conducive to conversations between generations.
5. Positive reinforcement: Encourage and appreciate effective

intergenerational communication.

Navigating age-melded terrains may seem tedious; however, intergenerational mixing can provide vibrant, diverse perspectives benefiting everyone involved. Remember, bridging this gap is not about changing who we are, but about improving how we express ourselves, thus connecting better, valuing differences, and creating harmonious relationships.

Chapter 8. Fostering Empathy Across the Generations

Understanding the importance of empathy in generational communication is crucial in building stronger relationships and bridge the generational gap. Empathy allows us to connect with others on a personal level, enabling us to comprehend their perspectives, feelings, and thoughts. It promotes tolerance, open-mindedness, and assists in the prevention of miscommunication. In cross-generational communication, these benefits are even more pronounced, as they can help alleviate misunderstandings that stem from the differing perspectives and experiences of each generation.

8.1. The Importance of Empathy in Cross-Generational Communication

Understanding the perspective of our elders, peers, or youngsters not only enriches our relationships, but also lends us vital insights to navigate our own lives. Acknowledging their wisdom and learning from their stories are often transformative experiences. From the practical tips of Baby Boomers, to the innovative contributions of Gen Z, there is knowledge to be gleaned from each generation.

On the flip side, showing empathy can offer important emotional support to the subject of our understanding. The feeling of being understood can alleviate feelings of isolation, particularly in individuals from older generations or younger ones who might feel misunderstood due to generational differences.

8.2. Developing Empathetic Awareness

To foster empathy, one must first develop a keen awareness of the other person's feelings. This might involve listening intently, watching for non-verbal cues, and paying mind to the context of the situation. These skills, though they might require some honing, can drastically improve one's ability to empathize.

Start with conversations. To fully understand someone's viewpoint, it's essential to converse with them. Ask open-ended questions and listen attentively to their answers. Make an active effort to engage and try not to pass judgment or draw conclusions prematurely.

Non-verbal cues, such as facial expressions, body language, and tone of voice, can also provide valuable insights into a person's emotional state. Learn to interpret these cues and react to them accordingly.

8.3. Understanding Generational Experiences

Each generation has distinctive experiences and world views shaped by their time. For example, Baby Boomers experienced significant economic growth and movements for social change, while Gen X was dubbed the "latchkey generation" due to socio-economic changes that led to an increase in single parent or two working-parent households. Millennials grew up with the internet boom and unpredictable economic fluctuations, whereas Gen Z is the first generation to be born fully immersed in the digital, hyperconnected age. These experiences naturally shape their values, behaviors, and communication preferences, making them somewhat alien to other generations.

To foster empathy across generations, we need to understand these generational influences. Educate yourself about the historical, socio-economic, and cultural contexts that shaped each generation. Understanding these contexts provides a foundation for understanding certain attitudes, behaviors, and perspectives.

8.4. Bridges, Not Walls: Encouraging Open Dialogue

One of the most effective ways to foster empathy is through an open dialogue. This type of communication involves a free exchange of ideas and understanding, and it encourages empathy by allowing each party to explore the perspective of the other.

The first step is to approach the conversation with a clear, open mind. Be respectful of each other's viewpoints and resist the urge to jump to conclusions. Active listening is also an essential component of open dialogue. Offer your full attention and fully absorb what's being said before responding.

Establishing ground rules can also help ensure that the conversation remains respectful and productive. Some possible rules might include, "No interrupting," "No judgment," and "Everyone's opinion is valued."

8.5. The Power of Storytelling

We are all unique, yet bound by the common thread of humanity. Our respective journeys, experiences, and viewpoints are stories waiting to be told. Sharing these stories can foster empathy by allowing each generation to put themselves in the others' shoes.

Encourage story sharing within your family, workspace, or community. It could be as simple as a weekly dinner table conversation or a formal story sharing event. This will promote bonding, solidify intergenerational relationships and pave the way for building a bridge over the generational gap.

In conclusion, fostering empathy across generations involves developing our understanding, promoting open dialogue, and facilitating shared experiences. By integrating these practices into our daily lives, we can bridge generational divides and contribute to even stronger communal bonds.

Chapter 9. Developing Effective Communication Strategies

Whether you're staring across a boardroom at a team of multi-generational professionals or puzzling over how to reach out to consumers spanning several demographic cohorts, developing effective communication strategies is crucial. In this segment, we'll delve deep into practical strategies to improve chasms in communication, engaging with members from Baby Boomers to Gen Z all the while enhancing understanding and solidifying connections.

9.1. Understanding the Gen Z

Being the latest generation to enter the workforce, Gen Z demands an understanding of their characteristics and communication preferences. Known for their comfort with technology, Gen Z individuals favor quick, succinct, and visually engaging communication.

Firstly, keep communications brief and incisive. Gen Z'ers are often seen as having a shorter attention span, so limiting email lengths and meeting durations can boost engagement. Also, understand that they're digital natives, gracefully juggling between multiple platforms. It's vital to utilize different communication channels such as social media, video conferences, or chat tools.

Lastly, make use of visual content. Gen Z'ers are drawn to infographics, emojis, quick explainer videos or any visual elements that can help convey a message quickly and creatively.

9.2. Engaging Millennials

Millennials, the generation that came of age during the internet boom, also favour speedy and efficient communication, with an added emphasis on authenticity. As a socially conscious generation, they appreciate transparency and a more relaxed, casual tone.

Open up a two-way communication channel - consider chat tools like Slack, which facilitate group conversations and direct messaging. Use language that's more on the informal side, minimizing the use of jargon and corporate lingo.

Moreover, stress value and purpose in your communications, as Millennials want their work to hold meaning. An approach emphasizing the 'why' behind requests or directives bridges this communication gap effectively.

9.3. Reaching Out to Gen X

Balancing a blend of traditional and modern communication styles, Gen X appreciates clear, concise communications - whether in email, phone call, or a face-to-face meeting. They value independence and might dislike being micromanaged.

In articulating your messages, aim for straightforwardness and efficiency – cut out the fluff. Use both digital and traditional communication methods, ensuring not to leave any essential details to the assumption. Lastly, provide them room for autonomy. Gen X'ers value their ability to work independently, so avoid unnecessary check-ins and give them the freedom they crave.

9.4. Communicating with Baby Boomers

Baby Boomers, largely relying on face-to-face interactions and phone calls, have adapted to digital tools, albeit at a slower pace than the younger generations. They emphasize personal relationships and respect formal lines of authority.

Ensure your communication is detailed and thorough, prefers in-person meetings or phone calls, whenever possible. Also, ensure your tone is respectful, using more formal language compared to other generations. Finally, Boomers value training: so, if you're introducing new communication tools or platforms, provide comprehensive guidance to ensure they're comfortable using them.

9.5. Cross-Generational Communication Strategies

While tailoring individual communication styles, it's vital not to pigeonhole every individual into their generational stereotype. There is always overlap and variation within generations, and your strategies should accommodate such nuances.

Begin with creating an inclusive communication environment. Foster a culture where each team member feels heard, valued, and comfortable sharing ideas. Make use of various communication tools and methods, integrating both traditional and digital channels.

Secondly, nurture empathy. Encourage team members to understand others' perspectives and the reasons behind their preferential modes of communication. Regular team-building exercises or cross-generational mentoring programs can help in this aspect.

Finally, the key to effective communication is feedback. Keep channels of feedback open and ensure it's a two-way street. This will not only enhance understanding but also help in continually refining your communication strategies.

Developing effective communication strategies across generations is not a one-size-fits-all approach. It requires awareness, flexibility, and an empathy-centric ethos. By acknowledging and appreciating the unique communication styles each generation brings to the table, you can facilitate stronger, more meaningful connections - indeed a potent matchmaking recipe for minimizing the cross-generational communications gap.

Chapter 10. Harmonizing the Multi-generational Workplace

The office is increasingly transforming into a melting pot of multi-generational talent. Different generational cohorts, from Baby Boomers to Gen Z, labor together, each possessing its own set of needs, motivations, and communication styles. How do we bring harmony to such a diverse cohort? In this chapter, we delve into unique strategies tailored to the different generations, fostering a more productive and cooperative workplace.

10.1. Recognizing Unique Generational Traits

To harmonize a multi-generational workplace, one must first grasp the distinguishing traits of each generation.

Baby Boomers (1946-1964) are known for their strong work ethic, competitive nature and personable communication style. They prefer face-to-face interactions and value respect and recognition in the workplace.

Gen X (1965-1980) are technologically astute, value work-life balance, and yield a pragmatic approach to work. They appreciate independence and prefer direct and straightforward communication.

Millennials (1981-1996) are tech-savvy, innovative, and value purpose and progression in their work. Millennials prefer digital communication channels such as email and social media but are open to face-to-face communication.

Gen Z (1997 onwards) are digital natives, entrepreneurial, and value transparency and inclusivity. They are comfortable with virtual teams and online coordination preferring communication via rapid, bite-sized content like texts and social chats.

10.2. Communication: The Crucial Connector

The variances in communication styles across generations could lead to misunderstanding. It takes patience and flexibility to listen, understand, and bridge these differences.

Baby boomers, with a penchant for personal relationships and respectful communication, value in-person meetings and phone calls. Provide them with detailed communication, including background, context, and specifics.

Gen Xers acquire a balanced communication approach, comfortable with both personal interactions and digital means. To connect effectively, give them concise, straightforward information, leaving room for their input and independence.

Millennials gravitate towards concise digital communication platforms but value feedback and open dialogue. Regular check-ins, responsive emails, or instant messages suit their communication style.

Gen Z, consistently connected digitally, expect quick, convenient communication. Utilize platforms like instant messaging apps, social media, and various collaboration tools for real-time interaction.

10.3. Creating an Inclusive Environment

An inclusive work environment recognizes and respects every generation's unique characteristics. Implement flexibility in working hours and locations, recognizing that Gen X values work-life balance while Baby Boomers often appreciate a traditional work week. Build a culture that encourages continuous learning, catering to Millennials' desire for personal growth and Gen Z's innovative spirit.

Promote transparency and communication open lines that cater to different styles and preferences. Incorporate traditional and digital formats to ensure that every generation feels valued.

10.4. Encouraging Cross-generational Mentoring

Cross-generational mentoring fosters understanding and collaboration. Pair a technologically advanced Gen Z worker with a Baby Boomer to exchange knowledge on technological advancements and interpersonal skills. Similarly, the entrepreneurial mindset of Gen Z could inspire a Gen X worker, while the Gen X's practicality could ground a Millennial's ambition.

10.5. Leveraging Generational Strengths

Recognize that every generation brings unique strengths. Baby Boomers offer years of experience and skill, Gen X brings adaptability, Millennials contribute digital savviness and collaboration, and Gen Z provides an entrepreneurial spirit and deep understanding of technology. When these strengths are acknowledged and leveraged, companies can maximize productivity and innovation.

10.6. Responding to Conflict

Conflicts may arise due to different values, working styles, and communication preference. Rather than avoiding these issues, companies must proactively address conflicts in a respectful and constructive manner. Encourage open dialogue, where each party feels heard and understood, and work towards a solution that respects each party's needs and preferences.

In conclusion, managing a multi-generational workplace may seem daunting initially, but with open-mindedness, understanding, and the right strategies, it's an opportunity to create a vibrant and productive environment. An effective multigenerational strategy promises not just a harmonious workspace, but also competitive advantages in attracting, retaining talent, and fostering innovation.

Chapter 11. Towards a Unified Future: Appreciating the Value of Each Generation

In a society as diverse as ours, there's no doubt that each generation brings its unique perspective to the table. Learning to appreciate the inherent value of these perspectives is the key to bridging the generational communication gap towards a unified future.

11.1. Understanding Generational Values

Each generation boasts a set of values largely influenced by the social, political, and economic circumstances surrounding their formative years. Baby Boomers, sandwiched between two world wars, grew up in an age where hard work and discipline were paramount. This shaped their predilection for a hierarchical system. Gen X, however, was raised in an uncertain period marked by divorce, economic struggles, and a lack of adult supervision, which led to their self-reliant and pragmatic approach.

On the other hand, Millennials grew up in a far more tech-savvy era, marked by the expansion of the internet, rapid globalization, and ongoing wars. Their life experiences cultivated their affinity for global-mindedness, diversity, and constant learning, all while craving feedback and a work-life balance. Lastly, Gen Z, raised during the Great Recession, display a pragmatic perspective of the world, yet they thrive on collaboration and are entrepreneurial-spirited.

A clear understanding of these differing values paves the way for striking the right chord in multi-generational communication.

11.2. Embracing Differences, Enhancing Collaboration

The first step is to acknowledge and appreciate these differences. Recognize, for instance, that a Baby Boomer might appreciate direct communication, while a Gen Zer may respond better to more collaborative and less directive approaches. This acknowledgment creates room for generational interplay where collaboration can be fostered.

11.3. Each Generation Has a Unique Strength

Baby Boomers, with their disciplined work ethic and expertise, can provide the stability and direction needed in any team setting. Gen X's self-reliance and resourcefulness has led them to be markedly adaptable, beneficial in today's fluid work culture. Millennials' global-mindedness, when combined with their continual-learning drive, allow them to bring innovation and modern solutions to the table. Gen Z's knack for technology and collaborative mindset can enhance communication and efficiency in a digital age.

Acknowledging each generation's unique strengths enables a more harmonious coexistence.

11.4. Encouraging Generational Knowledge Transfer

For genuine unity, we need to encourage generational knowledge transfers. This can happen in an informal mentor-mentee relationship or through more structured policies. Encourage older generations to share their wisdom and experience while urging younger generations to offer their newest skills and fresh perspectives. These exchanges can forge stronger ties across generations.

11.5. Fostering an Inclusive Workplace Environment

An inclusive work environment can utilise these values and strengths effectively. Recognize and respect each generation's preferred mode of communication- be it face-to-face meetings, emails, or instant messaging. Create flexible work policies that cater to each generation's desires– from a structured 9-5 schedule to a more flexible work-from-home alternative.

11.6. Bridging the Gap: The Role of Leadership

Leadership plays a crucial role in fostering this unified future. They should become generational translators, understanding each group's language, moving beyond the stereotypes, and finding common grounds that bind the team together. Leaders not only have the responsibility to utilize generational differences for the betterment of the organization but also to create an environment where everyone feels respected and heard.

11.7. The Synergy of Generational Diversity

A unified future lies in the synergy of generational diversity. Just as an orchestra requires the uniqueness of each instrument for a beautiful symphony, so too does our society require the value of each generation to create a harmonious existence. But remember, this unity doesn't mean uniformity — it means creating room for diversity to flourish.

Generational differences should never be a barrier to communication. Instead, they should be viewed as an opportunity to gain new insights, ideas, and approaches. Our differences make up a vibrant mosaic of experiences, skills, and perspectives, enhancing our collective ability to creatively solve problems and thrive. By understanding, appreciating, and leveraging these differences, we bridge the generational communication gap, solidifying our progress towards a unified future.

Made in United States
Troutdale, OR
01/17/2025